EARLY AMERICAN
JETLINERS

EARLY AMERICAN JETLINERS

Boeing 707, Douglas DC-8 and Convair CV-880

Ugo Vicenzi

MBI Publishing Company

This edition first published in 1999 by MBI Publishing Company,
729 Prospect Avenue, PO Box 1, Osceola, WI 54020-0001 USA.

© 1999 Ugo Vicenzi

Previously published by Airlife Publishing Ltd, Shrewsbury, England.

MBI Publishing Company books are also available at discounts in
bulk quantity for industrial or sales-promotional use. For details
write to Special Sales Manager at Motorbooks International Wholesalers &
Distributors, 729 Prospect Avenue, PO Box 1, Osceola, WI 54020-0001 USA.

Library of Congress Cataloging-in-Publication Data available

ISBN 0-7603-0788-1

Printed in Singapore

Contents

Introduction

On a warm summer's day at an airport, somewhere in the world, a procession of quiet jetliners appear high over the horizon on their glide path to the runway. Suddenly a black line is revealed among the succession of wide-body lights and the four columns of smoke associated with the first generation of jetliners becomes evident – an elegant and exciting plane is on the way. Despite their innovative shapes and powerplants, the first generation of American four-engined jetliners has been characterised by the smoke they trailed, leaving an unmistakable footprint in the sky. This phenomenon caused problems to the extent that the Airport of New York Authority prescribed a two-minute waiting period after a Boeing 707 or DC-8 had taken-off.

For a decade, from the first commercial service of a Boeing 707 in 1958 to the appearance of the Boeing 747, the king of air transport was this breed of American jetliner. All were characterised by the same basic layout of four turbojets under swept wings and by their abundant smoke emission. It was the time of the smokers! For the following decade they carried the burden of the majority of long-range services, until the increasing abundance of wide-bodies relegated them to cargo and marginal services. They gave air transport a great leap forward, dramatically cutting times and opening the way to mass air travel at unprecedented levels of comfort. The airlines of the day had the problems of the aircraft's spectacular cost and then filling their capacity that was sometimes twice that offered by the propliners they replaced.

The Comet and the Tu-104 were first to fly revenue services, but the airline industry didn't change significantly until the Boeing 707, the DC-8 and the CV-880 appeared. Suddenly, hundreds and hundreds of glorious piston airliners became obsolete and all airlines rushed to buy the new technology. I recognise the contribution the British industry made to jet operations, with the Comet and the VC-10, both fine and capable machines which carried many passengers during their time. However, I've never photographed those elegant products and until I realised that it was getting too late, infact it was already too late. I have tried to publish my collection of photographs, so British airplane enthusiasts must excuse me for this omission. All three aircraft featured offered excellent operating performances, being both reliable and exceeding their expected service life. Forty years after their introduction, over 500 airframes are still operational – a tribute to the finest design and workmanship. There was, however, a victim: Convair Aeronautical went out of the airliner business despite its product being loved by travellers and proving to be both rugged and reliable.

The engines grew in power and size several times during the evolution of this breed. Being the first generation of commercial jet engines, big advances in technology became available in a short time. Each new version offered more power, better fuel consumption, less noise and less visible smoke. The CFM56 on the DC-8-70, which is included in this book as a member of the DC-8 family, was certainly not renowned for being a smoker.

Watching the water injection-assisted take-off of one of the early Boeing 707s and DC-8s was an awesome spectacle, with smoke pouring from the turbojets and a bomber-like noise. However, it was also painful to see such short margins left for the pilots in the very long and slow climbing take-offs. I have never been an airline or airport worker. Most of the time I have devoted to my lifelong fascination with aircraft has been spent outside the airport fence, observing airliner movements. Every time I spotted those unmistakable four columns of smoke approaching or departing the airfield I felt a surge of excitement. This book is devoted to those whom this generation of charismatic aircraft has inspired a similar joy.

Douglas DC-8

In 1952 Douglas had to make some tough decisions. The company had to decide whether to accept the gamble of a turbojet airliner or to continue with the development of its successful propliners. After lengthy discussions it was decided to freeze development on its first jetliner, to be christened the DC-8. By then a mock-up had already been produced, with the classical four-engine configuration, but there was still a number of questions about the engines. All the existing turbojets were characterised by insufficient thrust (some of the preliminary drafts of both Boeing and Douglas even considered a six-engined airliner, like the B-47), high fuel consumption and a short interval between overhauls. Last but not least, their design costs were terrible.

The dominant market position of Douglas suggested a cautious pace of development. In 1952, the DC-6 was at the peak of its sales and the DC-7C was due to enter service in 1956. Therefore a very costly jetliner project was treated with little priority by the then largest supplier of airliners. This was not the case for Boeing, who had to take a life or death gamble to produce a jet tanker to replace its KC-97.

Yearlong hesitations between deciding on turboprop or turbojet propulsion created another delay and perhaps only the first flight in 1954 of the Boeing 367-80 (which would lead to the Boeing 707) demonstrated the inevitable trend towards long-range jetliners. This delay was never overcome and was initially responsible for the greater success of the Model 707 and the eventual emergence of Boeing as a leading producer of airliners.

First came the certification of the basic Boeing 707 without transatlantic range. Boeing was again first to introduce an intercontinental version, the turbofan engine and the cargo versions. By 1955 the DC-8 programme was the highest priority in Santa Monica and Douglas tried to reduce the Boeing lead by not producing an experimental model, utilising the first production DC-8 for test and certification. Later this machine was delivered to National and had a varied career, at one stage being the only DC-8 ever operated by Lufthansa.

The ace in the DC-8 history was the production of the Series 60, which boosted its sales to 263 airframes and put the DC-8 project in a positive economic light. Ultimately, however, production stopped at 556 airframes, compared with the 967 civil Boeing 707s produced, supplemented by hundreds of military C-135s – a huge success for Boeing.

The DC-8-61/63 at the time of entering service was the largest jetliner in the world, a fact which was emphasised by Flying Tiger Line which proudly applied a large 'Jumbo Jet' title on their fuselages. These titles were quickly deleted when an aircraft with the same nickname (but MUCH larger) appeared from Boeing.

Aviation analysts have discussed the premature cancellation of the DC-8 programme, but in fact the Series 70 was initially a Douglas project and would certainly have given the company a healthy order book. However, by then McDonnell Douglas was in a bad economic situation and a costly DC-10 project killed future developments and orders. Part of the Douglas team which designed the super Series 70 later left the company and formed Cammacorp, which successfully converted 110 airframes, giving the DC-8 a longer operational life than the Boeing 707. Looking at the project after forty years of operation, there was nothing wrong with the DC-8, which provided excellent service to many airlines and even offered a longer airframe life. Perhaps the only fault was the initial delay.

The first order came from Pan Am on 13 October 1955. The first flight was achieved uneventfully on 30 May 1958, a time when forty-two DC-8s were on order. Delta flew the first revenue service on 18 September 1959. Initially, the reputation of Douglas was such, that despite deliveries starting two years later than Boeing, the order book was favourable, with Pan Am ordering twenty Boeing 707s and twenty-five DC-8s. Pilots liked the superior handling characteristics of the Douglas product, but were critical of the speed compared to that of the Boeing jet, causing scornful nicknames such as 'Diesel Eight' or 'Douglas Late'. Eventually Pan Am sold its DC-8 fleet and became a Boeing 707-only operator, a decision which greatly affected the market potential. Future operators of both aircraft were numerous. Among the most significant we may count Braniff, Airlift, Flying Tigers, World, Seaboard World, Korean and Southern Air Transport. In the end most of them preferred Douglas.

Douglas, produced a conventional project with the DC-8. The most unorthodox feature was the wing, which provided an 'inverted' profile close to the wing root with a flat extradox to improve airflow at high Mach numbers. This feature was exploited in a test flight when a DC-8-43 became the only airliner to exceed the sound barrier.

The DC-8 never attracted interest from US military operators who were to give so much success to the Boeing 707. One of Douglas' most advanced studies was carried out for the AWACS competition, where the Santa Monica team participated with a DC-8-62 modified with the dorsal radome. This was later adopted by the E-3 and created the realisation of a full wood mock-up. However, there was no chance against Boeing. One DC-8-50 entered the roster of US Navy.

At a certain stage Douglas considered developing the DC-8 for the short-range market, as Boeing did with the Model 720. They designed a smaller DC-8 powered by four Pratt & Whitney TF-10As and with a capacity of ninety-two seats. The aircraft was christened the DC-9, a designation which was later applied to the successful family of twin-jets when more powerful engines became available. This caused the cancellation of the four-engine version.

On many occasions the DC-8 airframe proved its sturdiness and has become famous for operating over a very long service life. A famous accident happened to Alitalia DC-8-43 I DIWL when it was overflying Beirut during the Six Days War. An Air-to-Air missile hit the right wing causing a large hole. Fortunately, this didn't ignite the fuel tanks and the ailing DC-8 made it back to Damascus.

The aircraft's reputed ability as a cargo carrier has brought about the conversion of many airframes. With the Series 70 programme the DC-8 will certainly be the longest-serving among the first-generation jetliners, flying well into the twenty-first century.

The major characteristics of the different versions are:

DC-8-10	Initial version, medium-range for US domestic routes JT3C engines with water injection First flight 30 May 1958
DC-8-20	Enhanced take-off performance JT4A engines with water injection First flight 29 November 1958
DC-8-30	Long-range version with strengthened airframe and extended wing tips JT4A engines

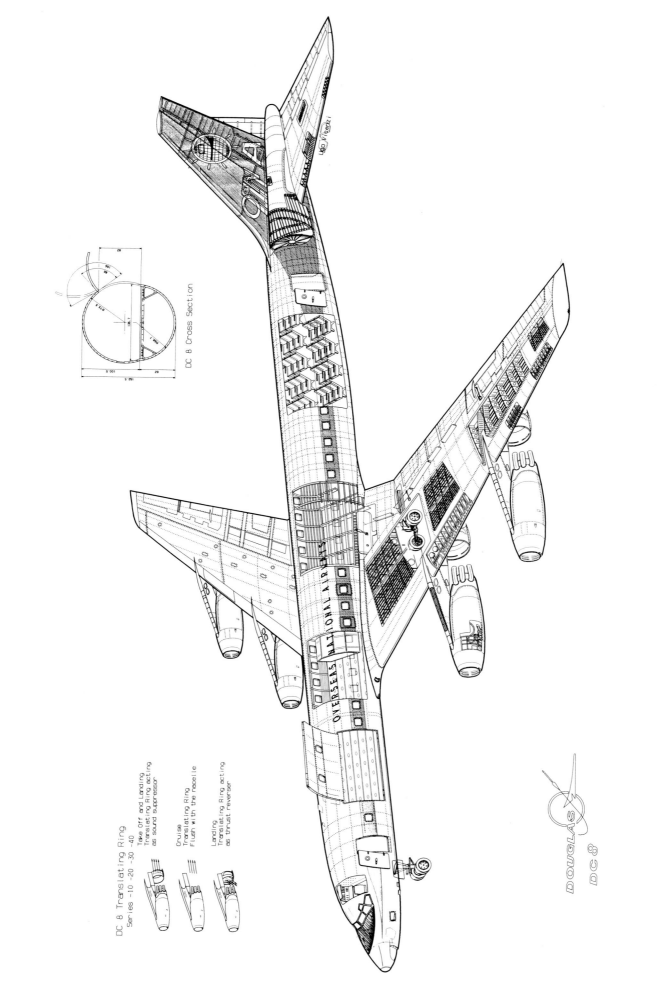

DC 8 Cross Section

DC 8 Translating Ring
Series -10 -20 -30 -40

Take Off and Landing
Translating Ring acting
as sound suppressor

Cruise
Translating Ring
Flush with the nacelle

Landing
Translating Ring acting
as thrust reverser

OVERSEAS NATIONAL AIRWAYS

Ugo Vicenzi

DOUGLAS
DC 8

DC-8-40	First flight 21 February 1950 Long-range version with strengthened airframe and aerodynamic improvements Rolls-Royce Conway engines First flight 23 July 1959	DC-8-62	Extended fuselage, but less than in Series 61 (6ft 8in) Aerodynamic changes, 6ft increase of wing span First flight 29 August 1963
DC-8-50	As Series 40 with JT3D turbofans First flight 20 December 1960	DC-8-63	Same aerodynamic improvements as Series 62 Same extension as Series 61 First flight 10 April 1967
DC-8-55	Cargo model, side-loading freight door and reinforced floor First flight 28 October 1962	DC-8-71,72,73	Converted Series 61, 62, 63 fitted with CFM56 turbofans.
DC-8-61	As Series 50 with fuselage extended to 36ft 8in JT3D turbofan engines First flight 14 March 1966		

BELOW: Two rivals, a DC-8 and Boeing 707 finally rest, awaiting their doom in the scrapyard in Kingman, Arizona. Hulks of early four-engined jets have been a familiar sight in many American airports since the early seventies. For many of them a limited payload and costly re-engining – or even conversion to freighter wasn't considered attractive. There was no way for Boeing 707s and DC-8s to escape a meeting with the smelter. The next time you drink a beer, try to imagine that the can may have over 60,000 flying hours on its flight log.

ABOVE: A couple of Airborne Express DC-8-61s share the cargo ramp of Los Angeles Airport, awaiting their nightshift.

N1805 was presented at the Salon de l'Aéronautique of Paris in 1973. The Dallas team of Braniff engineers had tried their best to interpret the design painted on a DC-8 model by Calder. The artist himself painted the final touches.

BELOW: With so many airlines now painting their aircraft in highly attractive colour schemes or using them as a means of publicity, the Braniff DC-8-62 livery designed by Alexander Calder would not attract much attention. However, in 1972 it attracted a lot of media coverage.

BELOW: Performing the famous turn on the final approach to Kai Tak Airport, an Evergreen DC-8-73 prepares to land at Hong Kong. The Cargo version of the Series 73 offers a 52-ton payload, only slightly more than the Series 63. However, it can perform shorter take-offs and there is also a 70% improvement in noise and no smoke.

OPPOSITE ABOVE AND BELOW: Along with United and Air Canada, Delta was one of the launch customers for the Cammacorp programme of modifications which produced the Series 70. One of Delta's DC-8-71s was photographed taking off from Miami runway 27L.

The Series 61 received the most benefit from the modification. Its payload was increased by over 16 tons, equalling that of a Series 63 or 73, with the same range and mileage cost. Furthermore, it matched the aerodynamic performance of the most modern DC-8s, with fuel consumption and speed benefits.

BELOW: In 1982 Alitalia disposed of its DC-8 fleet, which was put in storage at Marana. The two convertible DC-8-62CFs were the first to attract customers, soon finding their way into American skies. Many of the all-passenger types had brief careers in their original configurations, but were then converted to freighters. Conversions from passenger DC-8s usually offer a reduced payload, lacking the need for reinforced pavement of the full freighter type.

Alitalia operated the Douglas jet for thirty-five years, starting in 1960 with ten Series 43s and then acquiring ten Series 62s. After 1982 several Series 54Fs and 55Fs were leased from African operators in order to operate European cargo schedules.

OPPOSITE ABOVE: Gold rings on the engine inlets identify Series 50 and Series 61 DC-8s that comply with Stage 2 noise regulations. After the Stage 2 regulations came into effect most of these types, as well as the Series 62 and 63, had new nacelles and sound suppressors installed in order to continue services in the USA and many European countries. Nobody saw the business potential of offering a hush-kit for the Series 20s, 30s and 40s, thus condemning them to scrap or flights only in remote parts of the world, such as Zaire, now the home of many Stage 1 Boeing 707s and DC-8s. However, Air Zaire 90 CLG flies to many European destinations and so has had a hush-kit installed.

OPPOSITE BELOW: In the seventies Aero Peru adopted a unique pink-red livery. This airframe had an unusually quiet life, flown by a relatively small number of operators and remaining in its original DC-8-51 configuration. The aircraft's first owner was National Airlines, followed ten years later by Air Jamaica. After a five-year lease to Aero Peru it was bought by Capitol and retired shortly after.

BELOW: After many years of storage in Mojave this DC-8-33F found a way to pay some of its parking fees by taking a role in a minor Hollywood production. Later it found a buyer in Peru, Tocumen Air Cargo, arousing much speculation about what use would be made of a well camouflaged cargo aircraft on Peruvian airstrips. However, the aircraft crashed shortly afterwards near Iquitos.

OPPOSITE ABOVE: Pausing at Keflavik during a transatlantic flight is one of many DC-8s operated by the long-established Icelandic operator Loftleidr. At the time the photograph was taken (1983) the airline had been renamed Icelandair. This airline had a long and successful association with the DC-8, operating various DC-8-63s and 55s.

OPPOSITE BELOW: Cargo conversion extended the life of the first Alitalia DC-8-43, which found two new employers in South America. Aeronaves del Peru was the lessee when this photo was taken, and Aero Peru the owner. This situation is apparent by the Aeronaves livery on the right-hand side and that of Aero Peru on

To compensate for the slow winter business several convertible versions were employed and leased to operate cargo flights. Another service which was ideally suited for slack times was the operation of Hadj (Muslim pilgrimage to Mecca) flights on behalf of Middle East and African carriers.

the left. With the cargo often consisting of flowers there was seldom a weight limitation on Aeronaves flights. The airline's association with this machine ended when the aircraft hit Cerro Lilio Mountain, Mexico.

BELOW: The condition of this former Air Canada DC-8-43's airframe justifies its presence in the famed 'corrosion corner' of Miami. There was little demand for DC-8-43s after they were sold by the large carriers who initially ordered them. This particular example found an engagement one autumn operating Hadj pilgrimage flights on behalf of Libyan Arab and later operated some charter flights for Dominicana. However, it did not arouse any interest in other airlines and is seen here in its final months in 1980.

OPPOSITE: The nose of a DC-8 with its unmistakable air intakes gives a shark-like impression of aggressiveness. This nose belongs to a DC-8-55F of the Italian cargo operator Aeral, and still bears the red cheatline of its former employers, Swissair and Balair.

Air entering the upper and lower duct is conveyed to a turbocharger which controls the aircraft's air conditioning system, later being discharged in the first of the two outlets behind. The two systems work in parallel and one can partially use the other one in case of problems. The middle intake delivers air to a heat exchanger responsible for the cabin temperature, using the rear outlet to dispose of the redundant airflow. In the process which converted the Series 60s to Series 70s the upper and lower intakes became redundant and were faired, as well as the air outlets several metres behind. This improved the aerodynamics a little, but lost much of the characteristic appearance of this unique nose.

BELOW: Hispaniola is a cargo operator well known in Florida for its Douglas propliner operations. The airline attempted to start passenger operations in 1991 but experienced many difficulties and its DC-8-55 remained unwanted in Miami. The bright blue colours are derived from the former Canadian operator Holidair.

BELOW: The cold light of a November morning in 1989 shines on a smartly decorated DC-8-62 on the ramp at Zürich Airport. A group of Dominican pilots formed Antillana de Navegacion Aerea and started to operate a weekly charter from the Americas to Kloten, painting their aircraft in a green Iberia-like colour scheme. Competition was severe on this route and Antillana closed operations after only a handful of rotations had been completed. Some of the airline's pilots started a cargo operation named Antillas Air Cargo, again with an Iberia-like colour scheme applied on their DC-7C Seven Seas. Unfortunately, they were again unlucky, as their Seven Seas ditched off the coast of Miami.

LEFT: This flight engineer console is a reminder of the technology of the last prop liners. All the gauges for the four engines and aircraft systems, fuel management and so on would keep the engineer busy during the flight. In the early sixties a fourth crew member was present, acting as flight mechanic, until confidence with the new machine increased and new procedures were implemented.

BELOW: The perennial glacier of Monte Rosa acts as a backdrop for Aer Turas DC-8-63F EI-BNA, photographed taxying to the holding point of Milano Malpensa runway 35R. This mountain requires attention from the crew, as a fully loaded DC-8 has to perform a spiral in order to clear the 12,000-plus feet of this snowy giant. This aircraft was originally a member of the Flying Tiger Line fleet, the largest operator of freighter DC-8s until the appearance of UPS (United Parcel Service).

OPPOSITE ABOVE: In the early sixties many cargo aircraft had doors unable to accept bulky items, such as Rolls-Royce Conway or Pratt & Whitney JT3 engines. It was therefore common for DC-8s and Boeing 707s to carry the replacement engines under the wing in a specifically designed pod. A fairing on the intake prevented the engines from windmilling and improved the aerodynamics as demonstrated on this CP Air DC-8-43.

The pictured DC-8 is an historical airframe, as it was the first airliner to exceed the speed of sound. The occasion happened on a test flight in 1961 during trials of the new wing leading edge and was achieved during a steep dive. A plate on the cockpit commemorated this feat but wasn't enough to save the aircraft from being scrapped.

OPPOSITE BELOW: The pilot workplace of an Icelandair DC-8-63.

BELOW: Several years after disposing of its Boeing 707 fleet, Air France lacked an intercontinental plane to operate Caribbean flights in summer 1990. The best available machine was a DC-8-61. C-GMXB came from the defunct Canadian operator Nationair, hence the Canadian registration.

This was actually the second DC-8 in the Air France roster. In the summer of 1973 OO-TCP, a DC-8-33, was leased from the Belgian operator Pomair to operate European routes. Air France therefore entered the restricted circle of operators which employed both the Boeing and its arch rival from Douglas.

OPPOSITE ABOVE: Seychelles International DC-8-63 awaits 259 sun-seekers. The unobstructed fuselage certainly exploited the available space, but to the rear-seated passengers it emphasised the idea of a narrow tube. Until the Boeing 747 revolutionised aircraft interiors, this was the standard layout of the jetliners of the sixties and seventies. Early versions of the DC-8 were not equipped with overhead boxes for hand luggage.

OPPOSITE BELOW: The side shot is the view which epitomises the super-stretch of the DC-8-63, the longest of the family with its 57.12-metre fuselage. A further 5.5-metre stretch was envisaged by the Santa Monica designers for the Series 80, enabling another thirty passengers to be seated. However, the Douglas management preferred the completely new DC-10.

N907CL was leased by Icelandair to supplement its fleet in summer 1982 and for the short-term lease it was decided to retain the livery of the former operator, Capitol. This machine, which originally entered service in 1968 as a DC-8-63, later swapped its JT3D engines for the quieter CFM56s. It was converted to a full freighter Series 73F and used by UPS.

23

BELOW: Like the majority of customers who ordered the early versions of the DC-8, Air Canada remained faithful to the type. DC-8s were operated by the Canadian carrier when it was still named Trans Canada. The airline first used several DC-8-43s, then later used some Series 53s and 54Fs for cargo work. Both the super-stretched Series 61 and 63 were ordered. One example of the latter version was photographed in August 1982 at Pearson International Airport, Toronto. It had just arrived from Paris. The relationship between Air Canada and Douglas ended here, as the TriStar was preferred to the DC-10.

OPPOSITE ABOVE: 5Y-BAS was photographed landing at its home base, Basel-Mulhouse, with a full load of passengers from Mombasa. African Safari is rather unique as it is one of the few operators which successfully operates as a travel agency, tourist village operation and airline. In an increasingly specialised world where single-job companies seem to perform better than those offering the full range of services, this is remarkable. The fleet commenced operations with a Bristol Britannia and continued with a DC-8-33, a DC-8-53 and two DC-8-63s. African Safari remained faithful to Douglas later utilising a DC-10.

OPPOSITE BELOW: An Aviaco DC-8-52 comes to land in Milano Malpensa in 1977 with a planeload of holidaymakers from Palma.

ABOVE: Not a fugitive from a Boeing 747 book but a Pratt & Whitney JT3D-3B, ready for installation on a DC-8-61 at the Cargolux maintenance area in Luxembourg. The ailing DC-8 concerned was owned by United Air Leasing and was being readied for service after being stored for a couple of years in Laurinburg, North Carolina. On the front can be seen the starting air exhaust which during start-up created the sound nicknamed the 'mating call'.

LEFT: The characteristic smoke emission on take-off is demonstrated here by a fully loaded Balair DC-8-63. This version was the noisiest of the subsonic jetliners and also required the longest runways. It therefore became common to hear of two-minute take-off runs in the rarefied air of La Paz. However, the smoke produced was insignificant compared to what a DC-8-10 or Series 20 could produce. To improve take-off performance and increase the time in which maximum power could be applied, a mixture of water and methanol was injected into the combustion chamber. Water helped to keep the temperature within reasonable limits, but created a torrent of black smoke and a distinct increase in sound.

OPPOSITE BELOW: The sun highlights the translating ring of this DC-8-43 which is in the full retracted position used during take-off and landing. This ring was a unique feature of the DC-8-10,-20,-30 and -40 and provided both sound suppression and thrust reverse. While the aircraft cruised, the ring translated forwards, operating flush with the engine nacelle. During take-off and landing it translated backwards to reduce noise. Two clamshell doors were incorporated in the ring and acted as thrust deflectors during landing. OB-R1142 was photographed in 1978 in Miami during a period of operation for Aero Peru and Air Jamaica.

RIGHT: A view of the throttle, thrust reverse levers and engine instruments on the console of a DC-8-63.

OPPOSITE ABOVE: First seen in 1971, the 'Flying Colors' dark blue-light blue livery is one of several attractive colour schemes introduced by Braniff. It is here seen applied on a DC-8-51.

OPPOSITE BELOW: The Rolls-Royce Conway 12 powerplant was installed on the Series 40, initially ordered by Trans Canada, Canadian Pacific and Alitalia. The howl of the Conway at start-up was unmistakable and very exciting. It was caused by compressed air taken from an external compressor at the engagement with the turbine reduction gear. The spectacle was repeated at every start-up and inevitably caused curiosity and concern – an incredible difference from the anonymous start-ups of today's turbofans!

RIGHT: Canafrica Transportes Aereos was an eighties charter operator with the typical mission of conveying tourists to the famed Iberian resorts. This DC-8-61 was the airline's first aircraft and was followed by another Series 61 and a Series 71.

BELOW: Over twice the diameter of the JT3Cs installed on the DC-8-11, the SNECMA CFM56-2 engines on this DC-8-71 are hung from very low pylons in order to provide the necessary ground clearance. The DC-8-71 first flew on 15 August 1981 and was certified on April 1982. The Series 70 programme was designed by Douglas, but the company decided not to proceed with it. Several people involved in this project therefore founded Cammacorp to implement the rejuvenation programme which modified 110 DC-8s. The aircraft featured belongs to the French charter operator Point Mulhouse and bears the colours of its former owner, Overseas National.

LEFT: The fully deployed flaps in landing configuration demonstrate a peculiarity of the DC-8 – the flaps had to be altered as the engine was positioned so close to the wings. Initially, the landing gear offered an advantage over the Boeing 707 as it had non-interconnected wheels. This design allowed movement on small taxiways and required less space to come out of the parkings. This arrangement was later also used on the Boeing 707-300.

BELOW: With an excellent payload and ample availability on short-term leases, the stretched DC-8 was the standard workhorse for the Hadj pilgrimage flights in the seventies and eighties, leading to a variety of interesting names on the fuselages of leased aircraft. Luxair mechanics were photographed applying Air Niger stickers on this DC-8-61, leased from Icelandair, at Luxembourg Airport in August 1982.

OPPOSITE ABOVE: This Andes Aerolineas del Ecuador DC-8-55F was photographed approaching the threshold of runway 30 in Miami. The suffix 55F identifies the most appealing subvariant of the Series 50, featuring a reinforced landing gear and strengthened cargo floor. The JT3D-3B engines allowed a payload of 42,161kg, over twice what was offered by the cargo version of the Series 30.

OPPOSITE BELOW: This Scandinavian Air System DC-8-63 was photographed temporarily resting on the ramp at Stockholm Arlanda while a thunderstorm raged in the summer sky.

BELOW: On location at the destination of many European charters, a Scanair DC-8-63 taxies with the clean blue waters of Las Palmas visible in the background.

OPPOSITE ABOVE: Almost one-fifth of DC-8s produced became mainliners with United Airlines, which owned a total of 105 examples. With the exception of the DC-8-40 and DC-8-63 almost all types were operated and United was launch customer for many of the versions. The last type of the breed, a DC-8-71 is seen here taxying out of the terminal at Orlando. Here, protection against trespassers isn't enforced by high fences with barbed wire, but by an elegant canal sweeping round the terminals.

OPPOSITE BELOW: Trans Ocean was founded in the eighties to operate North Atlantic and USAF charters, reviving the name of a famous fifties operator. However, Trans Ocean's second incarnation was much shorter, hindered by wide-body operators in a highly competitive market where flying first-generation jetliners became increasingly unprofitable. One of the airline's fully laden DC-8-63s was photographed taking off from Stansted, bound for Bangor. It demonstrated one of the less prized characteristics of the Series 63 – the longest and noisiest take-off run among all jetliners.

RIGHT: Hail has scratched part of the white cockpit of CTA DC-8-71. Pilots are busy running through their checklists, preparing for a flight from Zürich to Recife.

OPPOSITE ABOVE: Connie Kalitta commenced cargo operations in the seventies in Detroit with a fleet of Beech 18s and was keen to invest in larger types during the boom period of parcel carriers. Connie is a lover of motors and fine technology, himself a former dragster pilot, and wanted a fleet of DC-8s. The airline first operated directly under its own name and later as a subsidiary carrier for the giants in worldwide distribution. The red and yellow livery adopted since the formation of the company appeared on many DC-8s and larger types such as Boeing 747s.

BELOW: A red and ochre 'Flying Colors' Braniff DC-8-52 at Miami in 1978.

OPPOSITE BELOW: This DC-8-33F was the first jetliner operated by the company owned by Mrs Jean Rich, which up to this time flew DC-6s and C-46s in the Caribbean. It was photographed whilst landing in Miami one December morning in 1983.

RIGHT: The front wheels of the DC-8 can be steered 45° in both directions.

OPPOSITE ABOVE AND BELOW: With a fleet of forty-eight DC-8s, United Parcel Service (UPS) ranks among the largest operators of the type and is the first operator of Cammacorp-modified DC-8s. Its aircraft are Series 71 or 73 versions.

BELOW: The layout of the main landing gear remained the same throughout the DC-8's production, although materials and cross-sections were improved to support the increasingly heavy take-off loads.

OPPOSITE ABOVE: Thrust reversing was achieved in DC-8-62s and DC-8-63s via two clamshell doors enclosed in the engine nacelle. The aerodynamic improvements introduced with these versions to reduce the drag characteristics of the earlier types comprised one of the most elongated engine pylons ever produced.

OPPOSITE BELOW: The cargo door size of all the DC-8s, including this Saudia DC-8-63CF, is 140 × 85 inches wide. The fuselage of the longest version can accommodate eighteen standard pallets. The four freight cranes in the lower fuselage, measuring 36 × 44 inches, can accommodate a further 2500 cubic feet of cargo.

BELOW: A gust of crosswind lifts the right wing of a United DC-8-71 landing at Stapleton, Denver. The DC-8 wing had a 30° sweep, compared with the 35° of the Boeing 707 and allowed improved manoeuvrability on landing.

OPPOSITE ABOVE AND BELOW: The eight wheels of the main landing gear raise the customary cloud of dust as a DC-8-63 leased to a local freight company by Arrow Air touches down in the early morning in San Juan with a full load of cargo on behalf of Federal Express. Later the merchandise will be transferred to many smaller freighters for distribution to the various points of the Caribbean. Meanwhile the DC-8 will pick up another 50 tons of cargo bound for mainland USA.

For many years Arrow Air has been active as a cargo and passenger charter operator. The company has also built a reputation as a supplemental certified carrier on behalf of the USAF.

BELOW: This scene could easily have come from the sixties, when the most advanced jetliners were four-engined 'smokers' which would approach airports with the characteristic four columns of smoke. Two DC-8s were photographed approaching Miami in 1992, a period when aviation authorities were trying to banish those sky-polluting aircraft.

OPPOSITE ABOVE: The smart Hawaiian colour scheme was a firm favourite. Hawaiian operated several Series 62s and a single Series 63 between the islands and the USA mainland, as well as on charters to Europe and flights on behalf of the Department of Defense.

Many of the Series 62 improvements were aimed at reducing drag. Modifications included a new leading edge and wing tips with a greater span. New engine pylons were also added, which protruded much further from the wing leading edge than on the previous versions. The fuselage was lengthened by 2.03m, allowing the aircraft to accommodate up to 189 passengers in all-tourist configuration.

OPPOSITE BELOW: Japan Air Lines had a long association with the DC-8, becoming the largest operator of the type outside the USA. The airline used forty-four Series 30, 50, 61 and 62 aircraft on domestic and intercontinental passenger and cargo services. The Japanese airline has the undesired record of losing the most DC-8 airframes (seven). Two cases in particular were very unusual. DC-8-61 JA8061 hit the lights on landing at Tokyo Haneda when the pilot decided to commit suicide, applying full reverse when still on the landing path. DC-8-53 JA8013 landed by mistake on an air-strip near Juha, having missed Bombay. It had to be dismantled on site as it was impossible to lengthen the runway to allow a take-off.

BELOW: An African Safari DC-8-63 was photographed whilst climbing in the Kenyan cobalt winter sky.

OPPOSITE ABOVE: The year is 1990 and Hawaiian N897OU sinks gently onto the Miami runway. It was the last year that the aircraft operated for the airline and she was later converted into an executive jet.

OPPOSITE BELOW: An Air Jamaica DC-8-61 was photographed whilst taking off with a high load.

BELOW: This DC-8-61 belonged to Spantax, one of the few operators to use both the DC-8 and the Convair jets. Other airlines to use both aircraft were Delta and Swissair.

OPPOSITE ABOVE: Seaboard World was a large DC-8 cargo operator which operated the most widely travelled fleet. The airline achieved the highest utilisation rate for its aircraft with a large number of leases, for which the convertible type was the most useful. This DC-8-61 usually spent the busy summer months carrying Loftleidr Icelandic passengers which explains the blue cheatline. For the rest of the year the aircraft served as a freighter for the American cargo operator. The aircraft was photographed in August 1975 in Milano Malpensa.

OPPOSITE BELOW: Stripped of its famed Calder colours, N1805 was painted in a more subdued terracotta colour scheme, one of the 'Ultra' colour schemes of the Texan carrier's first generation. It was photographed approaching Los Angeles in 1980.

BELOW: A power generator, air compressor and a string of trucks and ancillaries are available for Ferien Service DC-8-62, resting at Zürich Kloten. N1805 was once the Braniff work of art designed by Alexander Calder, but was unceremoniously scrapped some years after this photograph was taken.

OPPOSITE ABOVE: In 1979 an Atlantic Ocean crossing in a DC-8 was still a daily service. A CP Air DC-8-53 was photographed climbing out of Milano Malpensa, bound for Toronto.

OPPOSITE BELOW: An American International DC-8-61 crosses the threshold of Aguadilla. Recently hush-kitted DC-8s like this one have had the air compressor intakes on the nose faired as with the DC-8-70 conversions.

List of crashed DC-8s to February 1999

Reg.	c/n	Date	Type	Airline	Location
N8013U	45290	16.12.60	11	UNITED	New York
XA XAX	45432	19.01.61	21	AERONAVES DE MEXICO	New York JFK
PH DCL	45615	30.05.61	53	KLM	Lisbon
N8040U	45307	11.07.61	12	UNITED	Denver
I DIWD	45631	07.07.62	43	ALITALIA	Bombay
PP PDT	45273	20.08.62	33F	PANAIR DO BRASIL	Rio Galeao
CF TJN	45654	29.11.63	54F	TRANS CANADA	Canada
N8607	45428	16.02.64	21	EASTERN	New Orleans
CF CPK	45761	04.03.66	43	CANADIAN PACIFIC	Haneda
ZK NZB	45751	04.07.66	52	AIR NEW ZEALAND	Auckland
XA PEI	45652	13.08.66	51	AERONAVES DE MEXICO	Acapulco
XA NUS	45633	24.12.66	51	AERONAVES DE MEXICO	Lake Texcoco
PP PEA	45253	04.03.67	33	VARIG	Monrovia
N802E	45409	30.03.67	51	DELTA	New Orleans
CF TJM	45653	19.05.67	54F	AIR CANADA	Ottawa
N1802	45277	28.04.68	31	CAPITOL	Atlantic City
I DIWF	45630	02.08.68	43	ALITALIA	Cuirone
LN MOO	45822	13.01.69	62	SAS	Los Angeles
N8634	46021	17.10.69	63CF	SEABOARD WORLD	Stockton
SE DBE	45823	19.04.70	62	SAS	Rome Fiumicino
CF TIW	46114	05.07.70	63	AIR CANADA	Toronto
N785FT	46005	27.07.70	63AF	FLYING TIGER LINE	Okinawa
N4863T	45951	08.09.70	63CF	TRANS INTERNATIONAL	New York JFK
I DIWZ	46026	15.09.70	62	ALITALIA	New York JFK
N4909C	46060	27.11.70	63CF	CAPITOL	Anchorage
I DIWB	45625	05.05.72	43	ALITALIA	Palermo
JA8012	45680	14.06.72	53	JAPAN AIR LINES	New Delhi
EC ARA	45617	06.07.72	52	AVIACO	Las Palmas
JA8013	45681	24.09.72	53	JAPAN AIR LINES	Bombay
JA8040	46057	28.11.72	62	JAPAN AIR LINES	Moscow
HS TGU	45526	10.05.73	33	THAI	Kathmandu
N802WA	46146	08.09.73	63CF	WORLD	Mt Dutton
PH MBH	45818	04.12.74	55F	GARUDA	Colombo
CU T1200	45638	18.03.76	43	CUBANA	Havana
CU T1201	45611	06.10.76	43	CUBANA	Barbados
JA8054	46148	13.01.77	62AF	JAPAN AIR LINES	Anchorage
N8635	46050	04.03.77	63CF	OVERSEAS NATIONAL	Niamey
RP C803	45937	18.04.77	53	PHILIPPINE AIRLINES	Haneda
JA8051	46152	27.09.77	53	JAPAN AIR LINES	Kuala Lumpur
N8047U	45880	18.12.77	54F	UNITED	Salt Lake City
EC BMX	45930	03.03.78	63	IBERIA	Santiago
TF FLA	46020	15.11.78	63CF	LOFTLEIDR ICELANDIC	Colombo
N8082U	45972	28.12.78	61	UNITED	Portland
HB IDE	45919	08.10.79	62	SWISSAIR	Athens
OB R1143	45598	01.08.80	43F	AERONAVES DEL PERU	Mt Cerro Lilio, Mexico
N715UA	45386	12.09.80	33F	AERONAVES DEL PERU	Iquitos
JA8061	45889	09.02.82	61	JAPAN AIR LINES	Tokyo Haneda
JA8038	46160	17.09.82	61	JAPAN AIR LINES	Shanghai
N8053U	46010	11.01.83	54F	UNITED	Detroit
HC BKN	45754	18.09.84	55F	AECA CARGA	Quito
HK2380	45879	18.09.84	54F	LAC COLOMBIA	Barranquilla
N950JW	46058	12.12.85	63PF	ARROW AIR	Gander
5N ARH	45859	31.03.88	55F	ARAX	Cairo
N1809E	46107	06.07.89	62	SURINAM	Paramaribo
OB T1316	45384	10.08.89	33F	APISA	Iquitos
N730PL	46161	12.03.91	62F	AIR TRANSPORT INT/L	New York JFK
C GMXQ	45982	11.07.91	61	NATIONAIR	Jeddah
9G MKB	45860	15.02.92	54F	MK AIR CARGO	Kano
N794AL	45923	15.02.92	63F	BURLINGTON AIR EXPRESS	Toledo
OB1456	45272	28.03.92	33F	EXPORT AIR CARGO	Iquitos
HK3753X	45765	15.10.92	55F	LAC COLOMBIA	Medellín
N814CK	46127	18.08.93	61F	AMERICAN INT/L AIRWAYS	Guantánamo Bay
N782AL	45929	16.02.95	63F	AIR TRANSPORT INT/L	Kansas City

N43UA	45677	28.04.95	54F	FAUCETT	Guatemala City
Z WSB	45805	28.01.96	55F	AFFRETAIR	Harare
HK3979X	45882	04.02.96	55F	LAC COLOMBIA	Asunción
N812CK	45890	31.05.96	61F	AMERICAN INT/L AIRWAYS	Lima
9G MKD	45965	17.12.96	55F	MK AIR CARGO	Port Harcourt
N827AX	45901	27.12.96	63F	AIRBORNE EXPRESS	Narrows VA
N20UA	45942	07.08.97	61F	FINE AIR	Miami
EL WVD	45885	18.11.97	55F	COUGAR CARGO	Mwanza, Tanzania

```
Total DC-8-10 =   2
Total DC-8-20 =   2
Total DC-8-30 =   7
Total DC-8-40 =   7
Total DC-8-50 = 24
Total DC-8-61 =   7
Total DC-8-62 =   9
Total DC-8-63 = 13
Total DC-8-71 =   0
Total DC-8-72 =   0
Total DC-8-73 =   0
                 —
Total DC-8     = 71
```

List of destroyed DC-8s to February 1999

Reg.	c/n	Date	Type	Airline	Location
N8784R	45769	25.11.65	54F	TRANS CARIBBEAN	Miami
PH DCH	45383	29.06.68	53	KLM	Amsterdam
HB IDD	45656	13.09.70	53	SWISSAIR	El Khana
CF TIJ	45962	21.06.73	53	AIR CANADA	Toronto
N6164A	46144	23.03.74	63CF	AIRLIFT	Travis AFB
N8170A	45270	21.12.77	33F	CHARLOTTE AIRCRAFT CO	Lake City
CF TJE	45565	78	43	FAA	Destruction Test
N913R	46128	15.01.81	61	SAUDIA	Luxembourg
F BOLL	46096	03.10.84	63PF	UTA	N'Djamena
C GSWX	45388	04.86	33F	DUNWOODY LSG	Abbotsford

```
Total DC-8-10 =   0
Total DC-8-20 =   0
Total DC-8-30 =   2
Total DC-8-40 =   1
Total DC-8-50 =   4
Total DC-8-61 =   1
Total DC-8-62 =   0
Total DC-8-63 =   2
Total DC-8-71 =   0
Total DC-8-72 =   0
Total DC-8-73 =   0
                 —
Total DC-8     = 10
```

Boeing 707

'A sixteen million dollar gamble', as a Boeing manager described it, began with the Seattle company's decision to build a prototype of a jet transport for possible military and civil use. It was a gamble the company could ill afford to lose, but as so often happens, the biggest bet yielded the highest gain. The Boeing 707 revolutionised air transport and shook the airline industry. Boeing's presence in the airline industry had so far been limited to the 307 and 377, hard to classify as successes. However, 'with the Boeing 707 the world shrank' (a famous phrase of an enthusiastic Pan Am president) and the domination of the market began to shift from Douglas to Boeing, never to return.

The USAF request for a tanker to replace the purposeful but slow Boeing KC-97 Stratotanker was too tempting for Boeing, as the company didn't want to lose the monopoly in air refuelling. With the company concerned by the market potential of the Comet, the gamble started. A firm idea on the aircraft configuration was only achieved with the eightieth project, creating the Boeing 367-80 designation. The figure 367 was used to create confusion but was also a reference to the commonality in tooling and fuselage with the Boeing 377. The new airliner was however completely new, sporting a 35° sweep wing and sharing the technology from the B-47 and B-52. Above all, it had four J57 turbojets. Work proceeded quickly and the first flight was achieved on the thirtieth anniversary of Boeing, 15 July 1954. However, the Boeing 367 specifications weren't satisfactory enough for the customers, so another costly redesign was necessary to secure the first order. The USAF bought twenty-nine KC-135As. This aircraft differed from the Boeing 367 as it had a larger fuselage and has a flying boom installed, the integral refuelling device of C-97 fame, which made it a very successful tanker.

The C-135 still didn't satisfy airline buyers. Its airframe was satisfactory for military transport, but not acceptable in the world of fail-safe airliners. Boeing therefore had to produce another major redesign of the fuselage, which was enlarged and lengthened, producing the first Boeing 707, the Series 100. The powerplants used in the civil version were the Pratt & Whitney JT3C-3s, basically derated J57s. These shared with the military version the water injection system responsible for a plentitude of smoke and noise. A drawback of this device was discovered in training. The water tank allowed only one take-off, so pilot training was very slow and costly.

Pan American was the first customer, placing an order for twenty Boeing 707-121s. To the disappointment of Boeing, Douglas' reputation was such that the airline also ordered twenty-five DC-8s. Time reversed this initial score and Pan Am ended up with 124 Boeing 707s but no DC-8s. Throughout the production of the Series 100, sales were almost level with Douglas, and matters didn't change with the Series 200 built only for Braniff, which had more powerful JT4 engines. The 707 still lacked intercontinental range, so a third major redesign was in store. Time was however on Boeing's side and while Douglas was busy catching up with the initial development of the DC-8, the Series 300 of the Boeing 707 could be produced more quickly. The Series 300 had a longer fuselage to accommodate up to 195 passengers and employed the Pratt & Whitney JT4 engine; the trailing edge of the wing was also redesigned. Boeing was the first to take advantage of the new JT3D turbofan engine which greatly reduced both fuel consumption and noise level: this was a real sales booster, making the Series 300 a best seller.

The Boeing 707-138 was a special version created for Qantas, using a shorter fuselage than the Series 100, trading accommodation for a greater range. The Series 400 had the same characteristics as the Series 300, but was propelled by four Rolls-Royce Conway Mk 50s; despite the offer of more attractive costs and payload, it was only ordered by BOAC, Lufthansa, El Al, Air India and VARIG. Only the superior performances of the JT3D prevented potentially good sales. Boeing also offered the Model 720, a lighter 707-100 aimed at the short and medium range market. The wing was redesigned with a higher sweep and full length leading edge slats. Until the appearance of the Boeing 727 and the DC-9, offering similar performances but with fewer engines, the Boeing 720 was an interesting proposition – 154 were produced.

The Boeing 707 has become one of the most successful airliners of all times, and on countless occasions has had to prove its reliability. One particular flight which demonstrated its capabilities happened during the Angolan evacuation in 1975, when a TAP Boeing 707 was able to take off with 342 passengers crammed into every available space. With numerous freighters and military transports still active worldwide, it is likely that the Boeing 707's fiftieth birthday will see some specimens still in the air.

The major characteristics of the different versions are:

B-367-80	Experimental airframe with fuselage derived from a C-97 and used for most of the testing of the 707 family First flight 15 July 1954
B-707-000	Non-official designation used by some airlines to identify the B-720-100, not used by Boeing.
B-707-100	Initial version, medium range for US domestic routes JT3C engines with water injection First flight 20 December 1958
B-707-100B	Same as B-707-100, but with JT3D turbofan engines
B-707-138	Special version for Qantas. Fuselage shortened by 10ft. Enhanced range JT3C engines with water injection First flight 29 November 1958
B-707-200	Special version for Braniff with increased take-off performance JT4A engines First flight June 1959
B-707-300	Long-range version with lengthened fuselage strengthened airframe and increased payload JT4A-3 engines First flight January 1959
B-707-300B	Improved 300 with longer wing and curved wing tips JT3D-3 engines
B-707-400	Same characteristics as series 300 but with Rolls-Royce Conway 50B bypass engines First flight May 1959
B-707-700	Single airframe for SNECMA CFM 56 engine evaluation First flight 27 November 1979
B-720	Short and medium range version with lightened airframe and new wing JT3C-7 engines First flight November 1959
B-720B	Same as B-720 with JT3D-3 engines

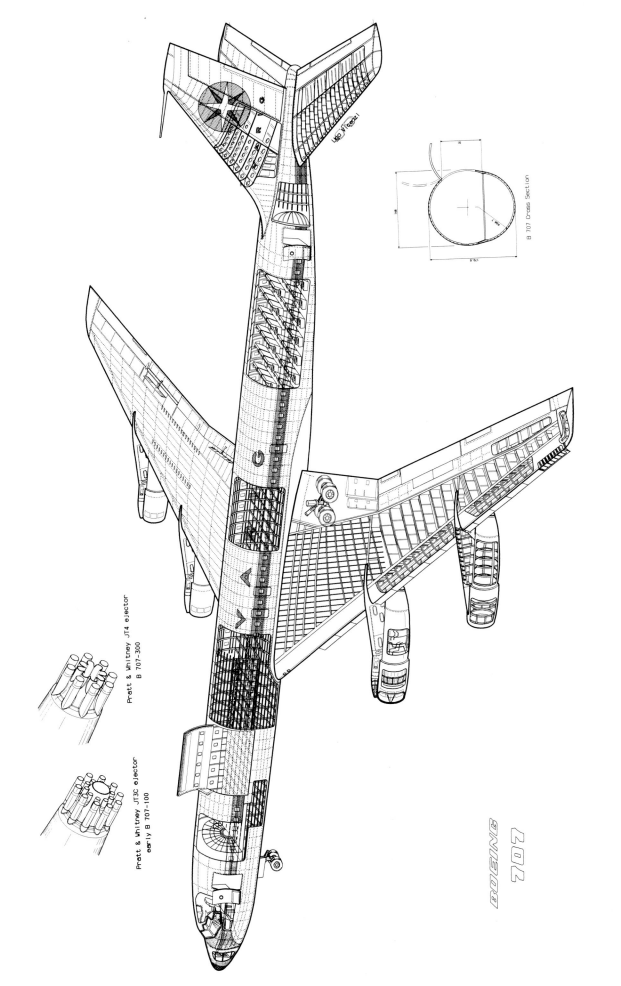

Pratt & Whitney JT4 ejector
B 707-300

Pratt & Whitney JT3C ejector
early B 707-100

B 707 Cross Section

BOEING 707

BELOW: The unmistakable green livery of Trans Mediterranean Airways (TMA) makes its Boeing 707s readily recognisable. In the heyday of Lebanon, TMA even started the first round-the-world cargo service, with its aircraft engaged in pick-up stops in a route circling the globe. With the Beirut crisis of the seventies these services were discontinued, but TMA remained active, using its distinctive Boeing 707s and several leased examples to carry loads from European destinations. Ostend was one of these destinations, where OD-AFY was photographed landing.

LEFT: The double lobe section of the Model 707 fuselage is evident from this head-on shot of a Race Boeing 707-300. The prototype Boeing 367-80 used an oval-section fuselage with the upper part the same as the C-97 (Boeing Model 367), which was later enlarged in the KC-135.

ABOVE: An Air France Boeing 707-328B was photographed whilst taking off in 1976, a period when the Model 707 jetliner was still flying the most important routes before the global usage of Boeing 747s. The suffix B on all Model 707s indicated those equipped with turbofan Pratt & Whitney JT3Ds, while the C suffix indicated cargo versions. As there was no BC combination, it was impossible to detect a turbojet or turbofan cargo Boeing 707 from the type designation alone.

BELOW: Thirty-seven Boeing 707s were produced as version 420s, with Rolls-Royce Conway engines having the same 7780kg thrust as the Pratt & Whitney JT3Cs. This installation achieved a similarly limited success on the DC-8 and the VC-10. The original customers for the Boeing 707-420s were BOAC, Lufthansa, Air India, VARIG and El Al.

ABOVE: A passenger view of the JT3D, the first successful turbofan engine, which was installed in over 1500 Boeing 707 and DC-8s and several hundred C-135s.

BELOW: The twilight of Boeing 707 operations should occur after the year 2000, when new noise regulations will prevent even the hush-kitted turbofan Model 707s from landing in the US and most European airports, unless an ultra-efficient hush-kit is designed that will certify them under Stage 3 noise rules. A different approach to extend the life of the many still young airframes lies in several re-engining projects currently under evaluation which employ quieter engines such as the JT8.

Boeing experimented by equipping the airliner with improved engines, and the last Boeing 707 produced was provided with the same CFM56 as the DC-8-70. However, Boeing decided not to proceed with the re-engining programme, which would have created the Boeing 707-720, as this would have affected sales of Boeing 757s. This test plane was used to gain experience on the re-engining of KC-135s and E-6s with the same powerplant.

RIGHT: The four columns of smoke from the Middle East Airlines Boeing 707 appear over the threshold.

OPPOSITE ABOVE: This Middle East Airline (MEA) Boeing 707-323C was photographed on approach to runway 36 at Milano Linate. The thin air enhanced the otherwise almost unnoticeable smoke trail of idling engines on a crisp day in March 1996. As well as reducing noise, the Dyna Rohr hush-kit employed on this Boeing 707 also affected the visible smoke. MEA has the distinction of being one of the last passenger Boeing 707 operators in Europe. With a grand total of forty Boeing 707s and 720s it could also rank among the largest operators of Boeing's first jetliner.

OPPOSITE BELOW: Advanced versions of the Pratt & Whitney JT3D engine installed on the Boeing 707 are equipped with six supplemental air intakes. These are opened on take-off to provide a smoother and greater flow of air, causing the typical shrill noise. These inlets are closed while the aircraft is cruising as less airflow is needed and drag reduction becomes more important. This African Express Boeing 707-344B has a red cheatline as a reminder of its past with Air Mauritius.

BELOW: This Rolls-Royce Conway Boeing 707 was photographed in the classic head-on shot, a trademark of the Boeing brochures. The subject of this photograph is a Boeing 707-436 of the charter operator Airwing. It was awaiting a possible buyer in Fort Lauderdale in 1984.

OPPOSITE ABOVE: The large root and the double sweep of the new wing introduced with the Series 300 are apparent in this photograph of a TAP Boeing 707-382. The Series 300 could accommodate 23,815 US gallons of fuel to enable intercontinental flights. The span was also increased by 12ft and the undercarriage was reinforced to accommodate the maximum weight of 335,000lb.

OPPOSITE BELOW: With a cargo door measuring 11' × 7.5', thirteen standard pallets can be loaded on a Boeing 707-320 to give a total load of 41,500kg, including the underdeck cargo area. The loading-unloading can be completed in less than an hour.
  The Boeing 707 was the first jetliner to employ slats on the wing leading edge to improve landing speeds, seen here in deployed configuration. The slats consisted of a series of fibreglass aerofoils bolted on an aluminium structure and proved so efficient that the design was not changed.

ABOVE AND BELOW: Only Santiago del Chile Airport was more frequently visited than Miami, where Fast Air Boeing 707-385C was photographed taking off. Boeing 707s were the backbone of the Chilean cargo operator during the eighties, but when a larger and quieter aircraft was required, the cargo fleet was supplemented with DC-8-70s.

Unlike most cargo Boeing 707s, which had very varied lives serving several worldwide operators, CC CEB had a faithful association with the Chilean carrier; it was delivered in December 1969 and only served with this operator.

ABOVE: Following a tradition dating from the Constellation period Trans World Airlines (TWA) also nicknamed its Boeing 707 with a star-associated name so the airliner became the StarStream 707. This Series 331, photographed taxiing at Milano Malpensa in the early seventies, remained with TWA until 1980, when it was sold to the Israeli Air Force. It was replaced by the Boeing 747-131, an aircraft which ended the tradition of 'stars' names. TWA was a large Boeing 707 operator, using a total of fifteen 131s and sixty-seven Boeing 331s; the 707s were used over a twenty-five-year period, longer than any other airline.

TOP: The heat reflected by Ostende's runway blurs the image of this Seagreen Air Transport Boeing 707-336C taxiing to the holding point, bound for Krasnodar.
(*Giuliano Provera*)

BELOW: A summer thunderstorm develops over the city of Sparta.
An Olympic Airways Boeing 707-384B was photographed parked
on the Milano Malpensa apron.

OPPOSITE ABOVE: Pan American was the first operator of both the Series 121 and 321. According to the Boeing tradition which started with the Model 707, the suffix 21 was allocated to Pan Am and every ordering airline received its own Boeing code, i.e. TWA was 31, BOAC was 38 and so on. This means that a Boeing 707-330B is not a special version, but a Series 300 originally delivered to Lufthansa. Pan Am was the largest operator of first-generation jetliners, using a total of eight Boeing 707-121s and 116 Boeing 707-321s.

OPPOSITE BELOW: Even among the fancy advertising colour schemes of the late nineties, the psychedelic colours applied to Boeing 707s and 720s in the seventies would not pass unnoticed. It is therefore easy to imagine what a stir they caused among the conventional cheatlines and metallic undersides of their contemporary airliners.

ABOVE: It is difficult to ascertain whether it was Avianca that adopted an Iraqi-like colour scheme or Iraqi that adopted an Avianca-like scheme.

OPPOSITE ABOVE: The Jomo Kenyatta airport tower, Nairobi, dominates the scene of summer afternoon in April 1981. Air Rwanda Boeing 707-328C, originally delivered to Air France, waits its passengers.

OPPOSITE BELOW: One of Lufthansa's original Boeing 707-430s was retired in 1975 after spending all its career with the German carrier. It was used as an apprentice trainer in Hamburg.

BELOW: When the Las Vegas casino and hotel Caesar's Palace was opened in the seventies, it saw the potential of an airliner conveying gamblers and tourists direct to the resort. With regulations favouring travel clubs, it was decided to purchase a Boeing 720-022 from United. It remained in operation for five months and was subsequently leased to the rock group Led Zeppelin, before becoming one of the many dismantled airframes to keep the fleet of USAF KC-135s alive.

OPPOSITE ABOVE: The weather was very humid when the sun appeared in the overcast sky over Stansted one afternoon in 1989. This caused a long condensation trail on a loaded Maof Boeing 720, bound for Basel and Tel Aviv.

OPPOSITE BELOW: Middle East Airlines (MEA) had a long association with the Boeing 720, using them on European and Middle East routes. The safety record was excellent and the maintenance was often carried out under war conditions. Unfortunately, MEA's fleet suffered much from the civil war in Lebanon, which caused the destruction of eight Boeing 720s and three Boeing 707s due to bombing.

BELOW: Airframes are cut in different ways, from the rough dismantling seen in non-specialised sites to the precise cutting using a large guillotine in Davis Monthan. People in Kingman are famous for their precise cuttings using torches such as in this operation. A view of the Arizona Desert can be seen through the fuselage of a former British Airways Boeing 707-436.

OPPOSITE ABOVE: The largest commercial aircraft operated in Nicaragua was this Boeing 720-051B, photographed landing in the colours of Aeronica in Miami. The Boeing 720 was intended as a medium-capacity jetliner for short-medium range, using a lighter Boeing 707 fuselage and systems. When more efficient twin-jets such as the Boeing 737 and the DC-9 were developed, the four JT3Cs of the Model 720 were no match. The Boeing 720's only asset therefore became its range and the so-called 'long and thin' sectors became its operational field.

OPPOSITE BELOW: Aeroamerica colours are evident on this Boeing 720-027, photographed whilst taxying at Milano Malpensa one torrid day in August 1975. At the time it was on lease to an airline named Ambassador International, operating inclusive tours in Europe. High-density configurations such as the one used here could accommodate 167 passengers and could provide good custom to the owners until more efficient twin-jets became available from leasing companies in the late eighties.

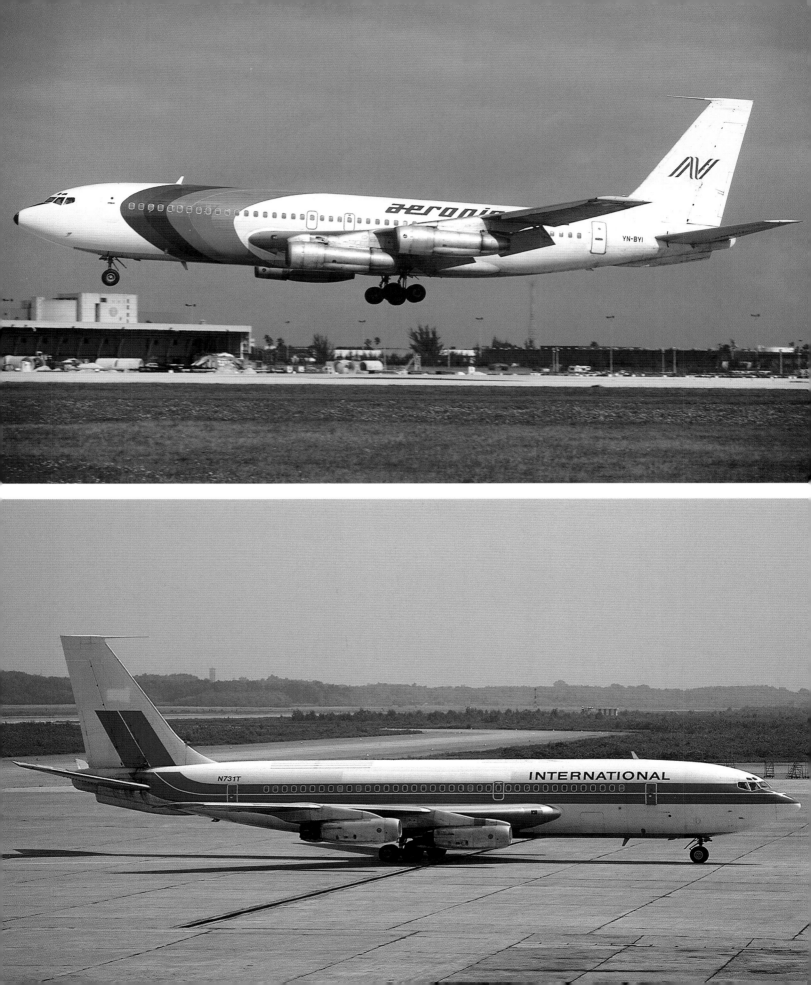

BELOW: Perhaps a lack of imagination gave the two Boeing 707s of the Pakistan Air Force the same military serials as their construction numbers. This original Northwest Orient Boeing 707-351C was photographed departing Geneva.
(*Max Fankhauser*)

OPPOSITE ABOVE: With a consignment of the renowned furniture from Cantu' (a furniture centre north of Milan) West African Cargo's single Boeing 707-336C takes off from Milano Malpensa in March 1973. After service with the Ghanaian operator this machine was to have many African owners, although always remaining Ostend-based.

OPPOSITE BELOW: There was a thick fog on the morning of 22 December 1975 when TWA Boeing 707-331B N18701 approached Milano Malpensa, but the crew decided to attempt the landing despite the advice of Air Traffic Control. The direction of the landing was correct, but outside the runway and in an almost parallel path. A famed casualty of the crash was the slightly injured Luciano Pavarotti. It was one unfortunate captain's last landing with TWA.

BELOW: A very old airframe, actually the fourth Boeing 707 built, had just received an engine change when this photograph was taken. It had swapped its original JT3C-6 turbojets with JT3D-3 turbofans and so received the 121B classification. The aircraft was captured on film in 1975 at Milano Linate Airport.

OPPOSITE ABOVE: One of Beech Aeronautical's products is the successful probe and drogue conversion for the Boeing 707, which becomes a KC-707, offering air refuelling capability to two aircraft at the same time. With the KC-135 not being manufactured for over twenty years, the conversion of cheap Boeing 707s attracted many air forces and extended the lives of many ageing 707s. Outside the USAF and *Armée de l'Air*, both operating C-135s, the only other flying boom refuelling method was found on the Iranian Air Force Boeing 707-3J9C. (*Eddy Gual*)

OPPOSITE BELOW: Among the most significative aircraft in aviation history is the Boeing 367-80, the venerable Dash 80 from which the family of Boeing 707s and C-135s originated. Before reaching its final destination at Boeing Field N70700 spent many years stored at Davis Monthan, where it is pictured here.

BELOW: This smart Colombian Boeing 707-123F of Aerocondor was photographed approaching Miami in 1976. It was one of the very few conversions of the Series 100 to freighter, due to the unattractive payload compared to a Boeing 707-300 or DC-8-50. (*Eddy Gual*)

OPPOSITE ABOVE: This Boeing 707-331F, photographed whil parked at Ostende in 1978, was one of the few Series 300 to ado a lower fin. The long-range Boeing 707s had a higher tail, b some also retained the lower fin.

OPPOSITE BELOW: African Express was a Kenyan chart operator which intended to operate flights from Mombasa to t major European destinations. However, it only managed to opera a weekly flight from Bergamo, with its aircraft lying dormant s days a week. The airline managed to survive for five years on th slim operation, using a variety of Boeing 707s, such as this form Jamahiria Boeing 707-321B.

BELOW: Transportes Aéreos Portugueses (TAP) received its first Boeing 707-382B, CS TBA, in December 1963. The airline operated Boeing 707s until 1988, using them for both passenger and cargo work. A Boeing 707-300 in all-tourist class configuration could accommodate up to 189 passengers, but a Portuguese Boeing 707 broke records by evacuating 342 people during the Angolan crisis of 1975.

PPOSITE ABOVE: Four JT3Ds await maintenance at Marana in ay 1980. This Boeing 707-123B was being readied for its elivery from American Airlines to Air Berlin USA. The Series 00, endowed with a favourable weight-to-power ratio, was the stest cruising Boeing 707, earning the nickname 'Hot Rod 707'.

OPPOSITE BELOW: No longer able to be used economically in passenger operation and cargo conversion also proving uneconomical, the only way to have a Boeing 707-100 in the air was to use it as a corporate or executive jet. This Boeing 707-138B, an original Qantas workhorse, was photographed awaiting its VIPs at Geneva, one of its typical ports of call. (*Max Fankhauser*)

BELOW: Perhaps imitating the successful series of Braniff Airways colour schemes of the seventies, the Danish operator adopted a pale blue wraparound livery on its Boeing 720-051B.

OPPOSITE ABOVE: During the 'Desert Storm' days it was impossible for the Kuwaiti airline to operate regular flights and so several of its aircraft were leased to other carriers, such as Trans Mediterranean Airways. The airline was leasing this Boeing 707, photographed landing at Bergamo.

OPPOSITE BELOW: The reason for this book – dense columns black exhaust are emitted from each Pratt & Whitney JT3 turbofan, screaming at their highest power setting. Most of th Ostend runway is being used during the heavy take-off. West Coa Boeing 707-336C was bound for its home base at Accra, Lagos.

BELOW: The last airworthy Boeing 707-400s found a niche in Zaire, where the absence of noise regulations and relatively cheap fuel offered the Conway-engined aircraft a last chance. New ACS was one such operator, able to fly the Boeing jetliner as long as the supply of spares from Rolls-Royce lasted.

OPPOSITE ABOVE: In the early seventies the unmistakable background of Hong Kong wasn't as crowded as today, permitting this view of the picturesque mountain ridge of the New Territories. While a Flying Tiger Line freighter awaits its line-up clearance, a Malaysian Boeing 707-320 has just started its take-off run, requiring all the power available from its JT3D turbofans. Fortunately the aircraft is at sea level, otherwise in the hot and humid climate the runway length would pose some weight limitations.

OPPOSITE BELOW: VARIG has the distinction of being one of the few major users (together with Air France) of all three types of first-generation jetliners featured in this book. The airline owned a substantial fleet of Boeing 707s, some DC-8s and three Convair 990s, which were inherited from an order of the merged airline REAL. The Brazilian operator didn't want to have so many aircraft types in its fleet, but for once Convair was able to have the order honoured. The only other operators to use all three types, on a smaller scale, were Bahamas World and Inair Panama. This Boeing 707-323C was photographed in 1980, awaiting its pallets in the cargo ramp of Milano Malpensa.

BELOW: D2-TOJ is a Boeing 707-349C originally delivered to Flying Tiger Line, a freight operator which started the jet age with Boeing 707s but became a large cargo DC-8 user. Unlike the first owner of this airframe, Linhas Aereas De Angola tested a DC-8 but later standardised its fleet with several used Boeing 707s.

OPPOSITE ABOVE: During 1978 German Cargo commenced operations with four Boeing 707s. For fourteen years the famous 'curry bombers' were familiar visitors to many European and Asiatic airports until the Boeing freighters were replaced by quieter and more capacious DC-8-70s, although unfortunately they were not painted in this attractive ochre colour scheme.

OPPOSITE BELOW: The nacelles of all the 'B suffix' Boeing 707 300s and Boeing 720s housed the Pratt & Whitney JT3D, the firs successful turbofan engine and installed in almost 1500 Boein 707s and DC-8s. The exhaust visible on the upper left comes fror one of the turbocompressors responsible for cabin pressurisatio and ventilation. The number of turbocompressors is an easy wa to differentiate a Boeing 720 from a Boeing 707: two of them ar present on the former and three on the latter.

RIGHT: Boeing 707 doors were the first to be equipped with inflatable emergency escapes, seen here housed in the lower part of the door of a VARIG Boeing 707-323C.

OPPOSITE ABOVE: The Boeing 707 cockpit provided seating for the pilot and co-pilot, with the flight engineer sat behind the co-pilot and the navigator behind the pilot. A further jump seat for the observer was available. The instrument layout remained almost unchanged over the near thirty-year production, and all the production panels were painted in Boeing 707 grey.

OPPOSITE BELOW: The conservative colour scheme of the last Boeing 707s of Ecuatoriana was captured in Miami in 1990.

BELOW: This photograph demonstrates the main landing gear of the Boeing 707 with the typical doors composed of two elements which remained in a faired position during take-off and landing.

RIGHT: The distinctive tail of the Boeing 707 was introduced with the later models of the Series 100 to improve stability. Almost all the original 'short' tails were replaced by this new one. Some Series 100 and some early Series 300 models had the long tail supplemented by a ventral fin to prevent over-rotation and to further increase longitudinal stability. With the introduction of the longer chord wing of the 'advanced' version the ventral fin became unnecessary and was no longer applied by Boeing. This fin belongs to a Libyan freighter.

OPPOSITE ABOVE: High over the Milano Linate threshold an Egyptair Boeing 707-300 lifts off.

OPPOSITE BELOW: The unserviceability of this Conway engine is evident from the blackbird nest. When this picture was taken there was only a handful of operational Boeing 707-400s with the original Rolls-Royce engines.

BELOW: Not just one of the 820 C-135s built, 53118 owns the distinction of being the very first KC-135 built for the United States Air Force in 1956. It was the subject of many publicity photographs as it was rolled out the same day as the last KC-97. It was still gleaming like brand-new when the camera captured it landing at Rhein Main Air Force Base thirty-four years later in 1990. No longer in use as a tanker, it was used as an airborne command post, classified as EC-135K and serving with the 552nd Airborne Warning & Control Wing.

OPPOSITE ABOVE: This photograph features the Las Vegas holding point for N7228U, a Boeing 720-022 operated by the Travel Club Atlanta Skylarks. This airframe ended its days in Peking, used as an instructional aircraft by the Civil Aviation Authority of China.

OPPOSITE BELOW: The short fuselage identifies this Cyprus Boeing 707-123B, photographed approaching its passenger tunnel in Zürich. Originally built for American Airlines in 1959 with JT3C engines, it was converted to 123B configuration in 1961 with the installation of JT3D turbofans.

BELOW: Among the 820 airframes produced, the only customer of the C-135 outside USA was the *Armée de l'Air*, which acquired twelve C-135Fs. The eleven remaining airframes, after one crashed in 1972, were converted to KC-135FRs with the installation of CFM56-2-B1 turbofans. The tail boom is here shown extended to its maximum length to use the probe adapter refuelling device.

List of crashed Boeing 707s and 720s to February 1999

Reg.	c/n	Date	Type	Airline	Location
N70773	17609	19.04.59	707/124	CONTINENTAL	Kansas City
N70775	17611	02.07.59	707/124	CONTINENTAL	Mt Carterville
N7514A	17641	15.08.59	707/123	AMERICAN	Calverton
N7502A	17629	28.01.60	707/123	AMERICAN	Long Island
OO SJB	17624	15.02.61	707/329	SABENA	Bruxelles
F BHSA	17613	21.07.61	707/328	AIR FRANCE	Hamburg
D ABOK	18058	04.12.61	720/030B	LUFTHANSA	Ebersheim
F BHST	18247	20.02.62	707/328	AIR FRANCE	Guadelupe
N7506A	17633	01.03.62	707/123B	AMERICAN	New York
F BHSL	17920	03.06.62	707/328	AIR FRANCE	Paris Orly
PP VJB	17906	27.11.62	707/441	VARIG	Lima
N724US	18354	12.02.63	720/051B	NORTHWEST ORIENT	Everglades
N709PA	17588	08.12.63	707/121	PAN AM	Elkton
N779PA	17904	07.04.64	707/139B	PAN AM	New York
D ABOP	18249	15.07.64	720/030B	LUFTHANSA	Ansbach
N769TW	17685	23.11.64	707/331	TWA	Roma Fiumicino
D ABOT	18463	24.12.64	707/330B	LUFTHANSA	New Delhi
AP AMH	18379	20.05.65	720/040B	PAKISTAN INTERNATIONAL	Cairo
N708PA	17586	17.09.65	707/121B	PAN AM	Antigua
VT DMN	18055	24.01.66	707/437	AIR INDIA	Mount Bianco
G APFE	17706	05.03.66	707/436	BOAC	Mount Fuji
N742TW	17669	06.11.67	707/131	TWA	Cincinnati
ET AAG	18454	09.01.68	720/060B	MIDDLE EAST AIRLINES	Beirut
N791SA	17698	07.02.68	707/138B	CP AIR	Vancouver
F BLCJ	19724	05.03.68	707/328C	AIR FRANCE	Point-à-Pitre
G ARWE	18373	08.04.68	707/465	BOAC	Heathrow
ZS EUW	19705	20.04.68	707/344C	SOUTH AFRICAN AIRWAYS	Windhoek
N798PA	18790	13.06.68	707/321C	PAN AM	Calcutta
OO SJK	19211	13.07.68	707/329C	SABENA	Lagos
N494PA	19696	12.12.68	707/321B	PAN AM	Caracas
N799PA	18824	26.12.68	707/321C	PAN AM	Elmendorf AFB
N787TW	18712	26.07.69	707/331C	TWA	Pomona
F BHSZ	18459	03.12.69	707/328B	AIR FRANCE	Caracas
N743TW	17670	22.04.70	707/131	TWA	Indianapolis
N790TW	18738	30.11.70	707/373C	TWA	Tel Aviv
VH DJI	17722	23.01.71	707/437	AIR INDIA	Bombay
N3166	19439	31.03.71	720/047B	WESTERN AIR LINES	Ontario
N461PA	19371	24.07.71	707/321C	PAN AM	Manila
AP AVZ	20487	15.12.71	707/340C	PIA	Urumchi
N15712	20068	14.09.72	707/331C	TWA	San Francisco Bay
SU AOW	19845	05.12.72	707/366C	EGYPTAIR	Beni Suef
CF PWZ	18826	02.01.73	707/321C	PACIFIC WESTERN	Telford Lake
JY ADO	20494	22.01.73	707/3D3C	ALIA	Kano
PP VLJ	19106	09.06.73	707/327C	VARIG	Rio de Janeiro
PP VJZ	19841	11.07.73	707/345C	VARIG	Paris Orly
N417PA	18959	23.07.73	707/321B	PAN AM	Papeete
N757TW	18395	16.01.74	707/131B	TWA	Los Angeles
N454PA	19376	30.01.74	707/321B	PAN AM	Pago Pago
N446PA	19268	20.04.74	707/321C	PAN AM	Bali
N37777	18044	22.04.76	720/022	INAIR PANAMA	Barranquilla
N8734	20063	11.09.74	707/331B	TWA	Ionian Sea
JY AEE	18767	03.08.75	707/321C	JORDANIAN WORLD	Agadir
N18701	19878	22.12.75	707/331B	TWA	Milano Malpensa
OD AFT	18020	01.01.76	720/023	MIDDLE EAST AIRLINES	Saudi Arabia
F BHSH	17620	07.09.76	707/328	AIR FRANCE	Campo del Oro
N730JP	17671	14.10.76	707/131F	LLOYD AEREO BOLIVIANO	Santa Cruz
SU AXA	20763	25.12.76	707/366C	EGYPTAIR	Bangkok
G APFK	17712	17.03.77	707/436	BRITISH AIRTOURS	Prestwick
G BEBP	18579	14.05.77	707/321C	IAS CARGO	Lusaka
OQ CRT	17718	09.08.77	707/430	PEARL AIR	Sanaa
ET ACD	19736	19.11.77	707/360C	ETHIOPIAN	Roma Fiumicino
OO SJE	17627	15.02.78	707/329	SABENA	Tenerife

HL7429	19363	20.04.78	707/321B	KOREAN	Murmansk
HL7412	19715	02.08.78	707/373C	KOREAN	Tehran
CC CCX	18584	03.08.78	707/351B	LAN CHILE	Ezeiza
PP VLU	19235	30.01.79	707/323C	VARIG	Pacific Ocean
5X UAL	18580	04.79	707/321C	UGANDA AIRLINES	Kampala
D ABUY	20395	26.07.79	707/330C	LUFTHANSA	Rio de Janeiro
5B DAM	17628	19.08.79	707/123B	CYPRUS AIRWAYS	Bahrain
B1834	18887	11.09.79	707/324C	CHINA AIRLINES	Chuwei
AP AWZ	20275	26.11.79	707/340C	PIA	Jeddah
HK725	18087	27.01.80	720/059B	AVIANCA COLOMBIA	Quito
B1826	20262	27.02.80	707/309C	CHINA AIRLINES	Manila
OO SJH	18890	11.05.80	707/329C	CAMEROON AIRLINES	Douala
HK2410	17605	20.12.80	707/321	AEROTAL COLOMBIA	Bogatá
AP AXK	18590	08.01.81	720/047B	PAKISTAN INTERNATIONAL	Quetta
PP VJT	19322	11.06.81	707/341C	VARIG	Manaus
OD AGT	19213	23.10.81	707/331C	TMA	Tokyo Narita
VH DJJ	17723	27.06.82	707/437	AIR INDIA	Bombay
ST AIM	19410	10.09.82	707/348C	SUDAN AIRWAYS	River Nile
SU APE	20342	17.10.82	707/366C	EGYPTAIR	Geneva
N8434	20173	04.12.82	707/323B	GLOBAL	Brasilia
5A DJO	18955	14.03.83	707/338C	JAMAHIRYA	Sebha
5N ARO	18924	25.09.83	707/336C	RN CARGO ASABIRI	Accra
N4465C	18411	14.10.83	707/436	COASTAL AIRWAYS	Perpignan
HK2401X	18707	14.12.83	707/373C	TAMPA COLOMBIA	Medellín
9Q CWR	18357	85	707/458	WOLF AVIATION	Kinshasa
TY BBR	20457	13.06.85	707/336B	BENIN GVMT	Sebha
LV JGR	19961	27.01.86	707/387C	AEROLINEAS ARGENTINAS	Buenos Aires
PP VJK	19822	03.01.87	707/379C	VARIG	Abidjan
PT TCO	18932	11.04.87	707/330C	TRANSBRASIL	Manaus
N144SP	19209	13.04.87	707/351C	BUFFALO	Kansas City
HL7406	20522	29.11.87	707/B5C	KOREAN	Andaman Sea
D2 TOI	18975	02.88	707/349C	TAAG ANGOLA	Luanda
D2 TOV	18881	21.07.88	707/328C	TAAG ANGOLA	Lagos
5X UBC	19630	17.10.88	707/338C	UGANDA AIRLINES	Roma Fiumicino
5N AYJ	19168	14.12.88	707/351C	GAS AIR CARGO	Kom Omran, Egypt
N7231T	19572	08.02.89	707/331B	INDEPENDENT AIR	Santa Maria
PT TCS	19354	21.03.89	707/349C	TRANSBRASIL	São Paulo
6O SBT	19316	17.05.89	707/330B	SOMALI AIRLINES	Nairobi
5Y BBK	19872	07.11.89	707/351C	KENYA AIRWAYS	Addis Ababa
9Q CVG	19162	01.03.90	707/329C	KATALE AERO TRANSPORT	Goma
ST ALK	18976	07.07.90	707.349C	TRANS ARABIAN	Khartoum
Et ACQ	19820	25.07.90	707/379C	ETHIOPIAN	Addis Ababa
N320MJ	20028	20.09.90	707/321B	COMTRAN INTERNATIONAL	Marana
St SAC	19377	04.12.90	707/321B	SUDANIA AIR CARGO	Nairobi
YR ABD	21651	10.01.91	707/3K1C	TAROM	Bucharest
A20 103	21103	29.10.91	707/368C	AUSTRALIAN AIR FORCE	Bridgetown
5A DJT	18888	09.12.91	707/351C	LIBYAN	Tripoli
ST ALX	18715	24.03.92	707/321C	GOLDEN STAR	Athens
9G RBO	18746	09.04.92	707/351C	GAS AIR CARGO	Lagos
PP TCP	19416	26.10.92	707/365C	TRANSBRASIL	Manaus
5X DAR	18825	25.11.92	707/321C	DAS AIR CARGO	Kano
OB 1400	19434	07.01.93	707/351C	AERONAVES DEL PERU	Lima
5N ARQ	18809	28.01.93	707/338C	DAS AIR CARGO	Nairobi
T96	19238	31.01.93	707/387B	LINEAS AEREAS DEL ESTADO	Recife
5N ABK	20669	20.12.94	707/3F9C	NIGERIA AIRWAYS	Hadejia, Nigeria
YR ABN	19379	17.08.95	707/321C	AIR AFRIQUE	N'Djamena
HK3355X	18886	09.10.95	707/324B	TAMPA	São Paulo
4K 401	19584	30.11.95	707/323C	AZERBAIJAN AIRLINES	Baku
5X JON	20546	30.06.96	707/369C	DAS AIR CARGO	Bamako
SU AVX	20760	21.08.96	707/366C	EGYPTAIR	Istanbul
N751MA	19582	22.10.96	707/323C	MILLON AIR	Manta, Ecuador
LV LGP	20077	23.10.96	707/372C	LADE	Buenos Aires
P4 OOO	19435	24.01.97	707/331C	FIRST INTERNATIONAL	Kinshasa
SU PBA	19843	10.03.98	707/336C	AIR MEMPHIS	Mombasa
5N VRG	19664	12.11.98	707/355C	RACE CARGO	Ostende

Total Boeing 707/100   =   14
Total Boeing 707/200   =   1
Total Boeing 707/300   =   93
Total Boeing 707/400   =   10
Total Boeing 720   =   10
                        ———
Total Boeing 707/B720 = 128

List of destroyed Boeing 707s and 720s to February 1999

Reg.	c/n	Date	Type	Airline	Location
N198CA	17661		707/131	CHARLOTTE AC	Mojave (film *Speed*)
PP VJR	19320	07.09.68	707/341C	VARIG	Rio de Janeiro
OD AFC	20225	28.12.68	707/384C	MEA	Beirut
N8715T	18917	13.09.70	707/331B	TWA	El Khana
N761TW	17673	08.03.72	707/331	TWA	Las Vegas
N458PA	19368	03.11.73	707/321C	PAN AM	Boston
N407PA	18838	17.12.73	707/321B	PAN AM	Roma, Fiumicino
OD AFX	19107	23.07.79	707/327C	TMA	Beirut
OD AGW	19440	07.81	707/327C	TMA	Beirut
OD AFR	18018	31.08.81	720/023B	MEA	Beirut
OD AFP	18017	12.06.82	720/023B	MEA	Beirut
OD AFW	18026	16.06.82	720/023B	MEA	Beirut
OD AFU	18029	12.06.82	720/023B	MEA	Beirut
OD AFB	20224	16.06.82	707/384C	MEA	Beirut
OD AGU	18938	16.06.82	707/323C	TMA	Beirut
OD AFO	18035	06.83	720/023B	MEA	Beirut
N60651	17928	06.84	707/344	COLUMBIA PICTURES	
N833NA	18066	01.12.84	720/027	NASA	Edwards AFB
OD AFL	18034	21.08.85	720/023B	MEA	Beirut
OD AHB	19588	08.01.87	707/323C	MEA	Beirut
B2402	20714	02.01.90	707/3J6B	CHINA SOUTHWEST	Guangzhou
ET AJZ	19433	25.03.91	707/385C	ETHIOPIAN AIRLINES	Asmara
CP1365	18692	31.08.91	707/323C	LLOYD AEREO BOLIVIANO	Dothan AL
OD AFY	19108	26.07.93	707/327C	TMA	Amsterdam
N138SR	17697	28.08.98	707/138	JAFFE GROUP	Port Harcourt

Total Boeing 707/100   =   1
Total Boeing 707/200   =   0
Total Boeing 707/300   = 16
Total Boeing 707/400   =   0
Total Boeing 720   =   8
                        ———
Total Boeing 707/720   = 26

Convair Jets

One of the less profitable projects in airliner history started in the mid-fifties with the relationship between the billionaire Howard Hughes and Convair. Accustomed to having a great influence on the aircraft designed for his partially owned airline TWA, Hughes obtained the power to influence Convair according to his wishes and this is reflected by some of the CV-880 specifications.

The cross-section of the fuselage has always been one of the most controversial aspects of the CV-880/990 family. Convair started designing configurations of six-abreast seats, as featured in the Boeing 707 and DC-8, but with a wider pitch for maximum comfort. Discussions with Howard Hughes consumed a lot of time, as he wanted a five-abreast configuration in order to have a smaller cross-section and so more speed. When the plans of both Boeing and Douglas became clear it was evident that Convair was very behind and so it was decided to pursue the short and medium-range market with a faster aircraft. Speed was to become the hallmark, but also the nightmare, of the Convair jet.

A controversial specification required the fastest airliner to be capable of taking off on 5000-ft runways in order to find a niche in the market; the wing therefore had a 35-degree sweep but also a very large area to allow short field performance. This specification proved to be rather short-sighted, as the Boeing 707 and the DC-8 were to be so widely used that even the small airports were improved to accommodate them. However, with a large wing there was space for large fuel tanks on the Convair, so the range was greater than on the original plans. The fuel tanks design took advantage of the experience gained with the F-102 fighter. The tanks were of integral type and maintenance free, the wing joints sealed by a film developed by 3M. Unlike the competition, engines were obtained from General Electric, which released its J79 of F-104 and Phantom fame for the civil market under the designation CJ-805.

The first customers were obviously the Hughes-influenced TWA, with thirty ordered, and Delta which ordered twenty. Business seemed to be going well when United authorised the purchase of the CV-880; Boeing was however quick to produce a domestic version of the Model 707, named the Model 720, and sold it at a favourable price. Boeing was therefore able to grab the important United order. The Model 720 ultimately wasn't a best seller, but damaged CV-880 sales, offering similar characteristics and being available earlier.

Convair improved the CV-880 in a new version, named CV-880M, which had an increased fuel capacity, more powerful CJ-805-3B engines and improved landing gear and flaps. New orders were, however, limited, the most important being a small number sold to Viasa and Japan Air Lines. Because these orders and the diminutive size of the fuselage, the CV-880 earned the nickname 'Japanese Boeing'.

A more substantial redesign was needed to secure an American Airlines order: the wing was redesigned and made slimmer to improve speed and leading edge slats were added to improve short field performance. A new turbofan engine was developed by General Electric which added a fan in the rear part of the engine and obtained a significant increase in thrust and a reduction in fuel consumption similar to the competitor's Pratt & Whitney JT3. The structure was also strengthened, producing the most sturdy jetliner. Convair was so anxious to gain the order of American that it signed a contract specifying the maximum speed and range, factor that proved costly.

The figure 990 was derived from the speed (in kph) just as the figure 880 was indicative of its speed (in feet per second). The new jet achieved far from the required results however and encountered drag problems over the wing. The solution came with the famous 'Kucheman carrots', named after the NACA engineer who developed them. The 'Kucheman carrots' were four separate pods over the wing which helped the airflow to separate smoothly. They could also be used to store fuel. This naturally caused delay as new prototype was made and aircraft had to be modified directly on the production line. American reduced its order from twenty-five to twenty but finally was able to operate the fastest jet airliner. The only other significant orders came from Swissair, which put eight CV-990s into service and SAS, which had two. Production of the Convair jets ended with only sixty-five CV-880s and thirty-seven CV-990s manufactured.

Both the CV-880 and CV-990 proved to be reliable and liked both by passengers and pilots and remained in service with the large operators until fuel prices increased to the point they became uneconomical to operate. With the exception of the TWA aircraft destined to lie in the Mojave Desert, most Convairs found second hand service with smaller airlines and travel clubs. The CV-880 and CV-990 were attractive because they were faster than aircraft operated by the large carriers and available at a low price. Some were converted to freighters, but the narrow fuselage and the limited payload made them of little use.

The last important roles came from government agencies. The US Navy employed a CV-880 for special duties and NASA operated two CV-990s for tests. In both cases the sturdiness of the airframe was to be used to advantage. NASA choose the CV-990 to test the landing gear of the Space Shuttle and installed it on the centre of the fuselage. It experienced many hard landings and even landed with deflated tyres, which would have posed serious problems to other jets.

Unfortunately, the time has run out for this family of attractive aircraft which ended the airliner operations of Convair. The major characteristics of the different versions are:

CV-880   Initial version, medium-range of US domestic routes
General Electric CJ-805 turbojets
First flight 10 August 1959

CV-880M Improved version with larger tanks and stronger landing gear
General Electric CJ-805-3 turbojets
First flight 3 October 1960

CV-990   Strengthened version, with lengthened fuselage and new wing
Increased fuel capacity on the wing bodies
General Electric CJ-805-23 turbofans
First flight 24 January 1961

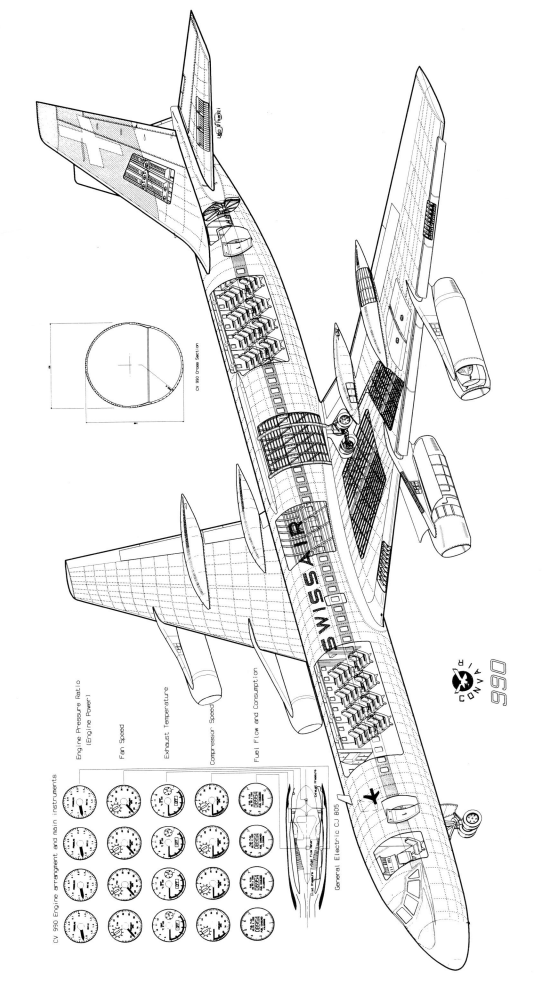

CV 990 Cross Section

CV 990 Engine arrangement and main instruments

Engine Pressure Ratio
(Engine Power)

Fan Speed

Exhaust Temperature

Compressor Speed

Fuel Flow and Consumption

General Electric CJ 805

SWISSAIR

CONVAIR 990

BELOW: Caracas-based operator Latin Carga leased a Monarch Airline converted CV-880 freighter in 1979. The airline was only able to operate it for eight months before a failed take-off destroyed the aircraft on 11 March 1980 at Caracas Simon Bolivar Airport.

OPPOSITE ABOVE: Lineas Aereas de Nicaragua operated six CV-880s over a five-year period in the seventies, connecting Miami and Mexico City to Nicaragua. The CV-880 was used because of Howard Hughes' involvement with the airline.

OPPOSITE BELOW: The largest collection of Convair jets was brought together after the retirement of Spantax's CV-990s in 1984, when eleven of the fourteen Coronados of the operator could be seen languishing at Palma.
(*A. Sastre*)

BELOW: Among the several airlines which shared an unlucky destiny with the Convair jet was Sunjet, which intended to operate the CV-880 in passenger schedules between Miami, St Kitts and St Martin. Plans failed to materialise and the former Lanica CV-880 remained stored at Miami.

OPPOSITE ABOVE: With a cargo door installed by American Jet Industries, Pan West CV-880 appeared to be one of the few Convairs able to fly out of Mojave destined for active service. Unfortunately, the fresh coast of paint was merely a way of earning cash from a movie production and was not from a new airline eager to start cargo operations. N375 was destined to stay in the desert.

OPPOSITE BELOW: Attracted perhaps more by the low purchas price of $1 million rather than the brisk performances, in 197 Elvis Presley became the owner of a CV-880, appropriatel registered N880EP. The aircraft was transformed into a luxur executive jet with beds, lavish armchairs, tables and gold-trimme furniture and bathrooms. After a short period of usage it becam part of the Graceland Museum of Memphis.

BELOW: The United States Navy became the last but not least important user of a CV-880 in 1980, when it acquired a rarely used Convair jet from the Federal Aviation Administration (FAA). Classified as UC880, it was fitted with the inflight refuelling system of the A3 Skywarrior and several antennas and radomes.

Quickly christened 'Old Smokey' by its crew, 161572 was able show its ruggedness in numerous special missions which took to bases worldwide. It flew until 1995, when the FAA used it test the effect of explosions on the controls and airframe. (*Eddy Gaul*)

OPPOSITE ABOVE: Palma was the last outpost of Convair jet operations and as late as 1984 it was possible to see several operational CV-990s on the tarmac. Spanish Air Taxi president Rodolfo Bay was a CV-990 enthusiast and responsible for keeping a fleet in the air when they were becoming less economical to operate. His fleet of fourteen CV-990s was only second to American Airlines' in size.
(*A. Sastre*)

OPPOSITE BELOW: The Spantax Convair could accommodat 149 passengers. An increased capacity was made possible by th new seats and upholstery specially designed by the Spanis operator. Improvements also included a new smokeles combustion chamber that greatly reduced the smoke produced b the CJ-850-23 turbofans and also benefited fuel economy. One c these 'advanced' CV-990s was photographed taking off from Base bound for Palma.

BELOW: Nomads Air Travel Club's first jet was this CV-990 from American and Modern Air. For six years it transported Club members to tourist destinations until replaced by a more efficient Boeing 727. The many flags on its fuselage are a reminder of when it was engaged in round-the-world flights.

OPPOSITE ABOVE: The independent South African State of Ciskei wanted to fly connections with neighbouring countries and in 1988 bought this former Denver Ports of Call CV-990. However, flight concessions weren't granted by the South African authorities and N8357C was only allowed to operate a sad 'inaugural' flight from Johannesburg. It then returned via Ostend to be stored in the United States to await another customer.

OPPOSITE BELOW: The colour scheme of this CV-880 belongs to the Hong Kong airline Cathay Pacific. The operator is a travel club named Travel a Go Go, which operated N48058 from 1976 to 1977. This airframe started its career with Swissair, which operated two CV-880s while awaiting the delayed delivery of its CV-990.

OPPOSITE ABOVE: King of the Smokers – the CV-880 left an impressive trail of smoke. During one of its very rare appearances in the air, the aircraft of Rainbow Air was photographed approaching Miami in a test flight.

OPPOSITE BELOW: An aspiring name sometimes isn't enough to assure success, which was the case of an American operator trading as Profit Express. The airline fell victim to the narrow fuselage of the CV-880. The standard cargo pallet couldn't be loaded and interchanged with other airlines, and the manual loading of freight coupled with the small payload caused any profit to remain mere wishful thinking.

LEFT: The fin of N990E, the former Nomads CV-990E, stands high in the Fort Lauderdale apron. A rather successful operation was carried out by Galaxy Airlines for several years, transporting gamblers to the casinos of Freeport, the Bahamas and Reno, Nevada.

ABOVE: After a thirteen-year career with Swissair, the twelfth CV-990 to be built was donated to the Swiss Transport Museum of Luzern and placed on permanent display. The closest airfield was the military base Alpnach, where HB ICC made its last landing on 20 March 1975. Transportation to the museum ended with spectacular crossing of the Vierwaldstätter See on 2 June 197 onboard an appropriately named barge.

List of crashed Convair 880s and 990s to February 1999

Reg.	c/n	Date	Type	Airline	Location
N820TW	22-00-26	16.12.60	880	TWA	Kansas City
N5616	30-10-28	30.05.63	990	AMERICAN	Newark
JA8030	22-00-45M	26.08.66	880M	JAPAN DOMESTIC AIRLINES	Tokyo
N8487H	22-00-37M	05.11.67	880M	CATHAY PACIFIC	Hong Kong
N821TW	22-00-27	21.11.67	880	TWA	Cincinnati
PK GJA	30-10-3	28.05.68	990	GARUDA	Bombay
JA8028	22-00-49M	25.06.69	880M	JAPAN AIR LINES	Moses Lake
EC BNM	30-10-32	05.01.70	990	SPANTAX	Stockholm
HB ICD	30-10-15	21.02.70	990	SWISSAIR	Zürich
N5603	30-10-13	08.08.70	990	MODERN AIR TRANSPORT	Mexico City
VR HFZ	22-7-1-53	15.06.72	880M	CATHAY PACIFIC	South Vietnam
EC BZR	30-10-25	03.12.72	990	SPANTAX	Tenerife
N8807E	22-10-29	20.12.72	880	DELTA AIR LINES	Chicago
N711NA	30-10-1	12.04.73	990	NASA	Sunnyvale, CA
N7876	30-10-4	09.10.73	990	CALIFORNIA AIRMOTIVE	Guam
N48060	22-00-47M	21.08.76	880M	AIRTRUST SINGAPORE	Seletar
N8817E	22-00-65	20.08.77	880	MONARCH AIRLINES	San Jose
N700NW	22-00-63	25.05.78	880	GROTH AIR	Miami
HP821	22-00-41	29.03.80	880	INAIR PANAMA	Panama City
YV145C	22-00-64	03.11.80	880	LATIN CARGA	Caracas
N712NA	30-10-37	17.07.85	990	NASA	March AFB

Total CV-880   = 7
Total CV-880M   = 5
Total CV-990   = 10
                     —
Total CV-880/880M/990 = 22

Appendix

DC-8 Production & Status (February 1999)

Type	Number built	Number modified (*)	Currently operational	Currently retired	Currently broken up	Currently destroyed	Currently crashed
DC-8-10	29						2
DC-8-20	34	16		4	43		2
DC-8-30	57			10	33	2	7
DC-8-40	32			9	12	1	7
DC-8-50	142	20	37	51	46	4	23
DC-8-61	88		21	6		1	7
DC-8-62	67		41	9	1		9
DC-8-63	107		40	1		2	13
DC-8-71		53	52	1			
DC-8-72		7	6	1			
DC-8-73		50	48	2			
Total	556	146	245	94	135	10	70

(*) from other versions

DC-8 Characteristics

	DC-8-10	DC-8-20	DC-8-30	DC-8-40	DC-8-50	DC-8-61	DC-8-62	DC-8-63	DC-8-71	DC-8-72	DC-8-73
Length (m)	45.87	45.87	45.87	45.87	45.87	57.11	47.98	57.11	57.11	47.98	57.11
Span (m)	43.41	43.41	43.41	43.41	43.41	43.41	45.24	45.24	43.41	45.24	45.24
Height (m)	13.21	13.21	13.21	13.21	13.21	13.11	13.21	13.11	13.11	13.21	13.11
Empty weight (kg)	55,928	58,967	60,781	62,460	58,377	67,540	63,185	66,361	70,800	67,100	73,500
Max weight (kg)	120,202	125,192	140,614	142,882	142,882	147,418	151,953	161,025	158,757	151,953	161,025
Max payload (kg)	17,735	17,367	19,278	19,552	42,161	32,613	41,141	52,027	52,027	41,141	52,027
Max cruise (kph)	900	964	946	941	954	935	945	959	959	945	959
High density pax	176	176	176	176	176	259	189	259	259	189	259
Engine type	P&W JT3C	P&W JT4A	P&W JT4A	RR Conway 12	P&W JT3D-3	P&W JT3D-3B	P&W JT3D-3B	P&W JT3D-7	SNECMA CFM56-2	SNECMA CFM56-2	SNECMA CFM56-2
Engine thrust (kg)	5,897	7,620	7,938	7,938	8,165	8,165	8,165	8,618	9,979	9,979	9,979
Range at max payload (km)	6,950	7,500	7,410	7,040	4,440	6,035	9,640	7,240	7,485	11,620	8,950
Max range (km)	6,920	7,710	9,605	9,817	11,100	11,500	11,610	11,300	12,390	13,675	12,390

Boeing 707 Production & Status (February 1999)						
Type	Number built	Currently operational	Currently w.f.u.	Currently broken up	Currently destroyed	Currently crashed
Boeing 707-100	138	6	8	108	2	14
Boeing 707-200	5			4		1
Boeing 707-300	583	211	91	163	16	93
Boeing 707-400	37		8	44		10
Boeing 720	154	6	34	96	8	10
Total	917	223	141	415	26	128

Note: several Boeing 707s have been converted to military variants and aren't included in this table

Boeing 707/720 Characteristics								
	707-100	707-100B	707-200	707-300	707-300B	707-400	720	720B
Length (m)	44.22	44.22	44.22	46.6	46.6	46.6	41.5	41.5
Span (m)	39.87	39.87	39.87	43.4	43.4	44.42	39.87	39.87
Height (m)	12.8	12.8	12.8	12.7	12.7	12.93	12.73	12.73
Empty weight (kg)	53,520	55,589	55,340	61,235	64,000	60,330	50,260	52,160
Max weight (kg)	116,575	117,027	116,575	143,335	151,315	143,335	103,870	106,140
Max speed (kph)	919	1,001	973	973	973	956	967	1,001
High density pax	181	181	181	195	195	195	167	167
Engine type	P&W JT3C-6	P&W JT3D-3	P&W JT4A-3	P&W JT4A-12	P&W JT3D-3B	RR Conway 508	P&W JT3C-12	P&W JT3D-3
Engine thrust (kg)	6,010	8,010	7,030	7,780	8,540	7,780	5,780	8,010
Max range (km)	7,485	8,485	7,485	10,860	12,030	10,840	8,430	9,950

Convair Jets Production & Status (February 1999)						
Type	Number built	Currently operational	Currently w.f.u.	Currently broken up	Currently destroyed	Currently crashed
CV-880	48	0	28	12	1	7
CV-880M	17	0	3	8	1	5
CV-990	37	0	13	13	1	10
	102	0	44	33	3	22

Convair 880/990 Characteristics			
	CV-880	CV-880M	CV-990
Length (m)	39.42	39.42	42.43
Span (m)	36.58	36.58	36.58
Height (m)	11	11	12.04
Empty Weight (kg)	39,645	42,638	54,840
Max Weight (kg)	83,690	87,540	115,645
Max Speed (kmh)	965	965	1,005
High Density Pax	124	124	146
Engine Type	GE CJ 805-3	GE CJ 805-3B	GE CJ 805-23
Engine Thrust (kg)	4,980	5,180	7,140
Max Range (km)	5,040	5,450	6,115